EIGHTH NOTE ♪ PUBLICATIONS

Suite
from Water Music

George Frederic Handel
Arranged by David Marlatt

George Frederic Handel (1685-1759) wrote three *Water Music* suites for performance by 50 instrumentalists on a barge during a royal procession on the Thames River in 1717. There are twenty-one movements in all ranging from slow airs to colourful allegros featuring two horns or two trumpets. The variety in tempos and the tuneful melodies have made *Water Music* a favorite of audiences since the first performance.

The four movements selected from the three Suites to form this new Suite are: *Minuet*, *Air*, *Allegro* and *Alla Hornpipe*.

ISBN: 9781771578431
CATALOG NUMBER: CC221135

COST: $20.00
DURATION: 7:20

DIFFICULTY RATING: Medium
4 Clarinets, Bass Clarinet

www.enpmusic.com

SUITE FROM WATER MUSIC

G.F. Handel
(1685-1759)
Arranged by David Marlatt

SUITE FROM WATER MUSIC pg. 2

SUITE FROM WATER MUSIC pg. 3

SUITE FROM WATER MUSIC

Bb Clarinet 1

G.F. Handel
(1685-1759)
Arranged by David Marlatt

SUITE FROM WATER MUSIC pg. 2

Bb Clarinet 2

SUITE FROM WATER MUSIC

G.F. Handel
(1685-1759)
Arranged by David Marlatt

SUITE FROM WATER MUSIC pg. 3

SUITE FROM WATER MUSIC pg. 2

SUITE FROM WATER MUSIC pg. 3

SUITE FROM WATER MUSIC pg. 2

SUITE FROM WATER MUSIC

Bb Clarinet 3

G.F. Handel
(1685-1759)
Arranged by David Marlatt

Bb Clarinet 4

SUITE FROM WATER MUSIC

G.F. Handel
(1685-1759)
Arranged by David Marlatt

SUITE FROM WATER MUSIC pg. 3

SUITE FROM WATER MUSIC pg. 2

B♭ Bass Clarinet

SUITE FROM WATER MUSIC

G.F. Handel
(1685-1759)
Arranged by David Marlatt

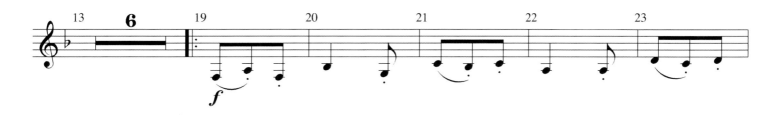

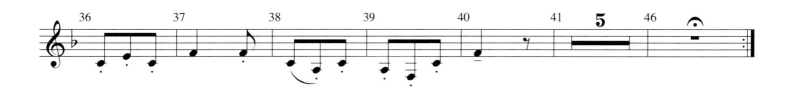

SUITE FROM WATER MUSIC pg. 3

SUITE FROM WATER MUSIC pg. 2

SUITE FROM WATER MUSIC pg. 8

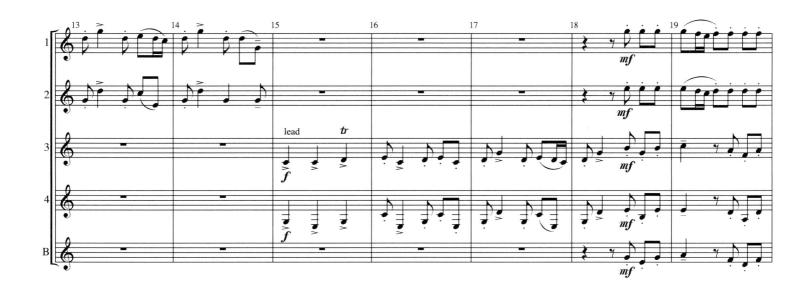

SUITE FROM WATER MUSIC pg. 9